Nebraska State Capitol

Omaha

Jane Moorman

There is a saying, "It was a Friday night and it seemed like a good idea at the time." That sums up the beginning of the State Capitols Project.

When photographer Jane Moorman told her brother of her idea of photographing state capitols, he said, "You do know there are 50 states and two of them you can't drive to."

Her answer was, "Your point is? It gives me a good reason to visit every state."

Nebraska: Unique governance

In true pioneer spirit, Nebraska's capitol reflects the independence of its leaders through its capitol building and unicameral legislature.

When the government outgrew its second capitol building, the present structure was constructed in the same location in Lincoln.

A first-of-a-kind architectural design was selected. Thomas Rogers Kimball, professional advisor to the capitol committee, wrote a design competition that did not dictate or even suggest a favored building style or form.

In response, New York architect Bertram Grosvenor Goodhue's design was selected. He modified and refined classical architectural design with an eye toward the simpler modern architecture coming from Europe at the time.

Construction of the non-traditional capitol building began in 1922. It took 10 years to complete the four phases that produced the final building. The lower section of the building is a square with a cross within it. Gardens are located in each quarter section.

The governmental offices are located in a 14-story tower at the center of the building.

Goodhue called on two artists who worked with him on other projects in New York City — Lee Lawrie and Hildreth Meiere. German-born Lawrie brought architectural sculpture into the modern era. Mosaic artist Meiere depicted the theme created by Hartley Burr Alexander, professor of philosophy at the University of Nebraska.

The theme throughout the building weaves the symbolism of the evolution of western democracy as a form of government paralleled with the natural and human history of Nebraska as a region.

Nebraska displaced with displays its independent thinking when it stepped away from the traditional two-chamber legislature.

In 1934, a unicameral system, commonly known as one-house legislature, was adopted to become more efficient and thus create cost savings.

The legislative body consists of 49 senators elected on a non-partisan basis.

Lincoln statue

Many states honor President Abraham Lincoln with a statue, but Nebraska is unique with the words of Lincoln's Gettysburg Address etched into the granite backdrop. The posture of the statue appears that Lincoln is pondering the meaning of those words.

Tower of the Plains

Nebraska was the first state to construct a capitol that was radically different from those with traditional domes.

Architectural styles of Assyrian, Egyptian, Roman, Greek and Gothic influenced the Roaring '20s art deco building designed by architect Bertram Grosvenor Goodhue.

The building's overall scheme draws upon the Great Plains for inspiration. Its broad, low base reflects the gently rolling hills of Nebraska and the tall tower depicts the other skyscrapers of the plains — grain elevators and church steeples.

The exterior of the building depicts the activities of the government conducted within. On the north façade are four figures representing wisdom, justice, power and mercy – traits of good governance.

Bas-reliefs carvings by Lee Lawrie represent all of Western Civilization with the Spirit of Law. The progression of the philosophical and political foundation of modern government is expressed with a series of reliefs — Law in the Ancient World, Written and Constitutional Law, and Spirit of Law in the New World.

Circling the tower base, the spiritual history of past ages is represented by leaders of its great periods.

The unity of the state's governing bodies is demonstrated with the name of each county carved on the exterior walls.

Golden Dome

The importance of agriculture in Nebraska culture is expressed in the design of the capitol's dome.

The 19-foot-tall "Sower" statue stands at the top of the gold-glazed tile dome 400 feet above the ground.

Lee Lawrie's figure is casting seed in the pre-mechanical method of sowing a field.

Circling the base of the dome are mosaics of the Native American figure "Thunderbird," the symbol for rain.

The Thunderbird is an important symbol for all Nebraskans, water being the key to agricultural production.

Honor To Citizens Who Build
A House Of State Where Men Live Well

The bison panels on the balustrades of the grand staircase illustrates the agricultural heritage of the Native Americans with corn in relief and the prayer honoring *"Mother Corn:"*

Arise with the dawn
Bathe in the morning sun
Sleep when the birds' no longer fly
Awake when the first faint dawn appears
Born of the earth
And touched by the deep blue sky
Out of the distant past I come unto you
Your Mother Corn

Above the capitol's main entrance is carved: "The salvation of the state is watchfulness in the citizens."

"The Spirit of the Prairie" mural by local Lincoln artist Elizabeth Dolan.

POLITICAL·SOCIETY·EXISTS·FOR·THE·SAKE·OF·NOBLE·LIVING
AKH NATON
SOLON
SOLO MON
JVLIVS CÆSAR
EZEKIEL

Vestibule

The theme of the capitol's vestibule is "Gifts of Nature to Man on the Plains."

The sun is represented at the top of the dome, in the chandelier, and on the large floor mosaic.

In the Guastavino mosaic tile dome, surrounding the sun and symbols featuring the four seasons, is a large circle showing the agricultural products of Nebraska.

The outer border of the dome contains the inscription: "Behold they come as householders, bringing earth's first fruits, rejoicing that the soil hath rewarded their labors with the abundance of its seasons."

The pendentives in the corners of the dome showcase the four seasons of agriculture. The arches surrounding the dome are filled with native animals of Nebraska.

Three wall murals, painted by James Penney, depict *"The Homesteader's Campfire,"* *"The First Furrow,"* and *"The House Raising."*

Foyer Theme: "Life of Man"

From the arched windows and ceiling to the floor, the Life of Man is depicted in mosaic art.

Circular mosaics in the ceiling represent past, present and future activities of society and all cultures.

Venetian glass wall murals were added to the hallway in 1967 to celebrate state centennial.

The hallway also includes the Nebraska Hall of Fame with busts of individuals who have served the state and nations.

Foyer Artwork

The foyer window arches contain figures to represent the activities of society: family, school, recreation, reflection, beauty, and truth.

The four inward-facing ceiling panels symbolize law, labor, public spirit and religion.

On the floor are three mosaics that represent the Earth: *The Spirit of the Soil, The Spirit of Vegetation, and The Spirit of Animal Life.*

The three medallions in the ceiling represent *Traditions of the Past, Life of the Present,* and *Ideas of the Future.*

The six large mosaics on the wall are: *The United States Survey* by Charles Clement, *The Blizzard of 1888* and *Tree Planting* by Jeanne Reynal, *The Coming of the Railroad* by F. John Miller, and *The Spirit of Nebraska* and *The Building of the Capitol* by Reinhold Marxhaussen.

Rotunda Tile Floor

Vital Energy is the theme for the rotunda floor design of black and white marble. The jet-black is from Belgium and the white is from Italy.

At the rotunda's center a large circular mosaic of *Earth as the Life Giver* is surrounded by four mosaics representing the *Genius of Water*, the *Genius of Fire*, the *Genius of Air* and the *Genius of Earth*. A mosaic band, or guilloche, interlaces the five circular mosaics and depicts the fossil life of the Great Plains.

Artist Hildreth Meiere based the fossil mosaics on scientific illustrations drawn by the University of Nebraska geologist Erwin Hinckley Barbour.

Rotunda Dome

Virtues which sustain society is the theme for the 110-foot-high rotunda dome. Forming a celestial rose within the mosaic dome are eight winged figures representing the virtues Temperance, Wisdom, Faith, Justice, Magnanimity, Charity, Hope, and Courage.

Hildreth Meiere created the mosaic. Meiere was a prolific art deco muralist whose highly styled figures and geometric patterns also adorned New York's Radio City Music Hall, the Great Hall of the National Academy of Sciences in Washington, D.C., and many other noted buildings. She did work on about 100 projects in 15 states.

Rotunda Art

Everywhere you look in the rotunda there is symbolic art — from the chandelier to the walls and floor.

Signs of the zodiac and sunburst encircle the 3,500-pound chandelier, which contains 136 light bulbs. The Native American motif theme is included with fans of arrows. Throughout the building, the light fixtures contain Nebraska symbols cast in bronze: corn, wheat, bison and arrows.

The Kenneth Evett wall murals represent the work of society to achieve virtue and noble life: *Labors of the Heads, Labors of the Hands, and Labors of the Heart.*

On the floor, the Earth Mother provides Nebraskans with food, water, and agricultural riches. The prehistoric life of Nebraska winds around Soil, Water, Fire and Air.

Labor of the Head

Labor of the Hands

Labor of the Heart

Acropolis of Greece

Capitol Hill in Rome

Mosaic Floors

The mosaic floors throughout the capitol were designed by Hildreth Meier. The Sunderland Brothers executed the inlaid three-quarter-inch squares of black marble and buff marble.

George W. Norris Legislative Chamber

The legislative chamber is home to the unicameral legislature.

The chamber represents Euro American expansion into the Nebraska region.

The chamber's tooled leather doors, designed by Hildreth Meiere, introduce the theme and depict a tree of life scene styled with Assyrian and Egyptian motifs.

Meiere also designed the gold leaf patterns on the walnut-beamed ceiling. The dominant images depict the three Euro-American powers that claimed the territory that is today Nebraska: Spain, France, and the United States of America.In 1984, the chamber was named for U.S. Senator George W. Norris.

AT THE PLATTE 1714

SIEVR DE BOVRG MOND

EDI T ION 1804

Warner Legislative Chamber

The former legislative chamber in the east section of the building was renamed the Warner Legislative Chamber to honor the Warner family and their contribution to the growth of the single-legislature unicameral system in Nebraska.

The chamber is used for ceremonial events.

The colorful mahogany doors to the chamber, designed by Lee Lawrie, tell of Native American culture and life.

The tree of life in the center of the doorway represents corn, the First People's main agricultural crop and important food source. The Thunderbird, a symbol of rain and life, is pictured at its center.

On the sides, a man is standing on an otter, a symbol of medicine, and a woman is standing on a turtle, the symbol of fertility.

Each door weighs 750 pounds. Lincoln artisan, Keats Lorenzo executed the carving.

Within the chamber, Hildreth Meire's ceiling mosaics represent the daily activities of the first culture of the Plains.

The mosaics and decorative borders were designed to look like Native American beadwork.

Governor's Office Suite

The decorative style of the Governor's Office Suite is Italian Renaissance.

New Yorker and muralist, Augustus Vincent Tack created the oil on canvas murals which simulate fresco.

The overall theme of the paintings is "Ideal Government and Ideal Life." They were installed in December 1927.

The Governor's Office Suite consists of the hearing room, reception room, secretary's office, and the governor's private office.

Separating the hearing room and the reception room is a large limestone fireplace decorated with carvings of bison and corn. On the hood is a crest featuring a pioneer woman and the state motto, "Equality Before the Law."

A large American flag is the backdrop for the hearing room.

Decorative details in the suite feature symbols of Nebraska's agriculture heritage.

TO CARE FOR HIM WHO SHALL HAVE BORNE THE BATTLE
AND FOR HIS WIDOW AND HIS ORPHAN

Memorial Chamber

Dedicated to the forms of heroism called in public service and devotion to humanity

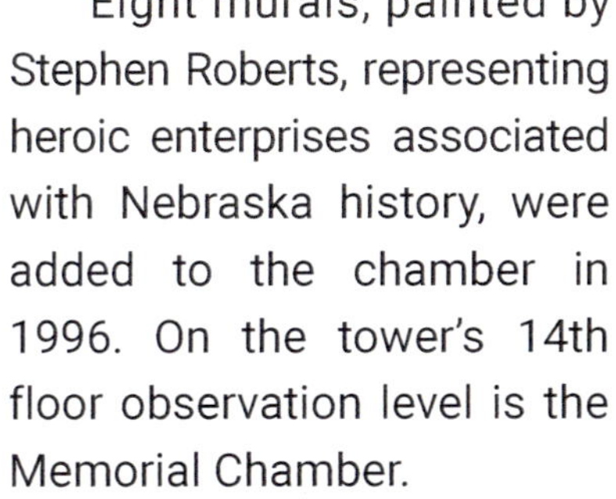

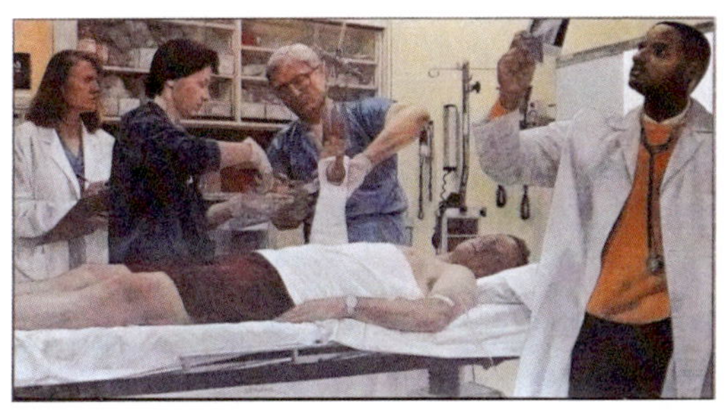

Eight murals, painted by Stephen Roberts, representing heroic enterprises associated with Nebraska history, were added to the chamber in 1996. On the tower's 14th floor observation level is the Memorial Chamber.

Inscription beneath the murals is taken from Abraham Lincoln's second inaugural address on March 4, 1865:

"With malice toward none with charity for all with firmness in the rights as God give us to see the right let us strive on to finish the work we are in to bind up the nation's wounds, to care for him who shall have borne the battle and for his widow and his orphan—to do all which may achieve and cherish a just and lasting peace among ourselves and with all nations."

Nebraska State Seal

The Great Seal of the State of Nebraska was created in 1867. Its design includes a steamboat ascending the Missouri River and a steam-engine-driven train traveling on the shore toward the Rocky Mountains, which are in the background.

In the foreground is a smith with a hammer and anvil, representing mechanical arts. Agriculture is represented by a settler's cabin, sheaves of wheat and stalks of growing corn.

In the sky above the mountains is the state motto: "Equality Before the Law." Surrounding the symbolic picture are the words, "Great Seal of the State of Nebraska."

The seal imprinted by a lion's head press was used for official business for 138 years. In 2005, Secretary of State John Gale retired the historic press.

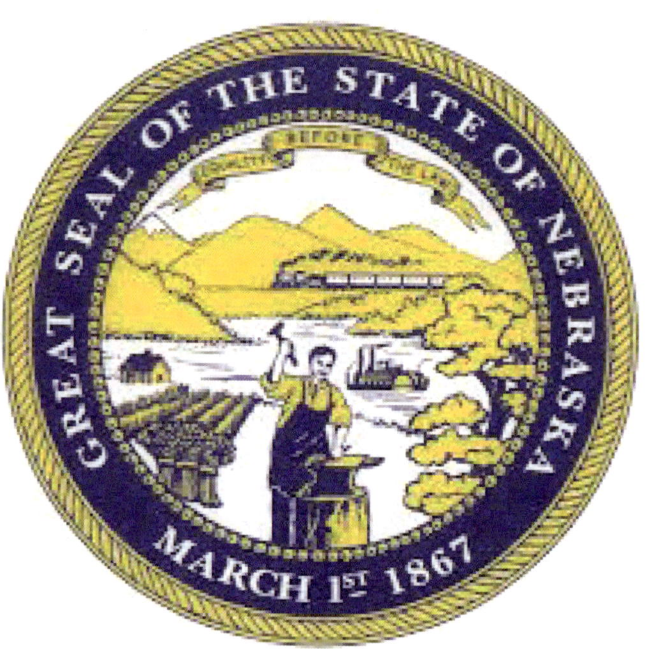

Column capital with horses, corn and wheat.

About the Photographer

Jane Moorman describes herself as an adventurer who loves to drive the backroads to see what there is to see.

During her 30-year journalism career, Jane honed her photography skills as a photojournalist, including covering high school sporting events.

A friend once said, "I wish I could see the world as Jane sees it. Finding the beauty in things that most of us don't take time to see."

Upon retiring in 2021, Jane decided there is a lot of her native country she had not visited, including each state's capitol, so she began her journey of exploring the USA.

She currently lives in Albuquerque, New Mexico, but says her real home is on the road.

www.ingramcontent.com/pod-product-compliance
Lightning Source LLC
Chambersburg PA
CBRC100836110726
48006CB00009B/1413